Love And In The Shadows Of

Rake E. Bond

BookLeaf Publishing

Presentation by *BookLeaf Publishing*

Web: www.bookleafpub.com

E-mail: info@bookleafpub.com

ISBN: 9789357214261

First edition 2022

This book is dedicated to all of the dreamers and artists who reside within each and every one of us. May all beings be in peace.

The Magi

Found myself spinning
In your elementary drive
But so stable
Your skin
Your eyes
Your lips
Dizzying
Yet so grounded and safe
A pencil in my hand
So I may live again
In my questions
And silence
I still found myself safe with you
The light I find home
Through your eyes
Making me feel
Everything I have suppressed
How do you do this so well?
I have fallen under your spell
And I thought I was the caster
I have been dreaming
And longing
For far too long

Humanity

We are so disconnected from who we are
My voice is in pain
Your voice is in pain
The echos of our ancestors travel far
Yet our world is so loud
We have not learned how to listen

The fire in my soul now
That rises from my core
And fanned by his longing
Or illusion of
Stirs me

To be desired, understood, loved,
And so deeply wanted
Is not this what we all crave?

Beneath the sorrows of our existence
Lies magic unseen
Wanting to be discovered

The Artist

Unspoken passion
Unsaid words left best for a sunrise
The temptation in the possibility
But life knows some things
Are best left to the imagination
Where nothing can be destroyed

Shall I leave this here?
Or find myself on a lonesome path
Only to become unraveled
In my daydream of temporary illusions?

Shall I love?
Or do I stay safe, right here.
With no one else ever again
To be the reason for my undoing

But he awakens within me
Art

All of which within me has been long lost

Agni

Rush in on some fated whim
Beneath the moon that is calling
Your perception settles me
Your depth and lightness
Stir my fire
Agni
Erotic fantasy
Take me to where I have never been
Taste me
My mouth is hungry
For your lips upon mine
And everything unspoken
From your eyes
Only you could ever do this
To my soul

Resurrection

Crescent hues
And ashes of wonder
I lay me down
Upon deaths door
Pale oak moss
Stable
Rooted through suffering
Watered by tears
Of my demise
And yet again
Risen
The chalice of life
I see you
Standing there
Your gaze upon my skin
Your beautiful throne
The world may never see
Your soul as deep
As the art
That echos in your voice
Speaking only to me
Stirring within me
The reason to remember
With just one glance
You tell me
All I need to know

Mirrors

Banish hollow
Prisoners
From my life
With the intent
To cripple and destroy
For they know not
Of their own doing
Unawakened minds
Whom I have had
The courage to seek
Meet and love
But only from the knowing
Of my then
Unawakened mind
Reflecting back to me
Everything I ever felt
I banish you
And the laughable untruths
I have ever believed
I do not love you
But I wish
For your peace
So you can no longer
Harm another soul
Including your own

The One

Perfect submission
To a man
So open and vulnerable
Fully expressed
And loving me
The way I always desired
To be loved
But was never ready for
Until this very moment

The Forgiven

Empty myself of everything
Because I am beautiful
Unlike you and the lies
Which have permeated my existence
Rid myself of myself
And your projections
Accusations
And words that have been daggers
To my soul
I forgive you
But can no longer reside
In the same space
For every day I have lived
I have strived to rise
And my energy must now
Be used to create
The life I desire
And wholly deserve

Fury

In the city of permanence
Where soot
Compromises the forgotten
Language of love
And entitlement pushes
Harrowing deeds
I remain unscathed
Compromises persuaded by gestures
And he was the jester
Spin me around
Not so merrily
Upon this wheel
Of divine discontent
And the breath of this masquerade
Has finally died

Freedom

Crashing into the sun
Lighting the last cigarette
Painful articulations
I cannot speak of
And can hardly muster the courage
To write
For that shall mean loss
Insurmountable
Again
Or would it
I have been cloaked
In my own destruction
The life of every artist
To know such pain
Or incredible joy
He makes me drop my defenses
As I put down the addiction
Smiled at my softer side
Holding me in a way
That I have never been held
I don't want to fall again
And lose everything
That makes me free
But he gives me the freedom
To explore it all

In the safety of our shared mutual understanding
And I begin to accomplish the things
I only dreamt of
But the prize was in the safety
And peace
And laughter
Kissing all of my wounds
So delicately

The One

He made love to me
Like nobody else
I could ever have dreamt of
Sensitive, soft, desire
Owned completely
He touched my mind
Glorified my heart
And exasperated my body
In peace I fell asleep
And in peace
I awoke
I am glad I stayed
The hallmark of a man
Who no longer needs to be raised
Emotionally aware
And as beautiful as one could come

The Sacred

Creation springs forth
From sexual desire
And action
Embody your sensual energy
Do not inhibit that
But
Do not give it away freely
Use it to create
Feel it rise up
From your pelvic floor
To your heart
Where all is sacred
Stirring around in your chest
Expanding out into the world
Rise
Awaken and fully embody
The glorious light
Of your illuminated body
Ethereal
Connected
And eternally
The ocean that is all
You
Beautiful soul
Are worth it

City

Once upon the city waves
In ashes of gold
Can I make you stay
But no
It's not my life
Being pulled from the fire
Crimson covered fairy dust
Upon hot coals that I rust
Falling for feigning
And gone tomorrow
I am going home
To the place
Where beauty swirls
In calm
Waters
Cleansing my soul
Of everything
That was never for me

Divine Essence

In truth I know
I am never alone
Another time
Another place
I remember when you held me near
Iridescent hands
Light glow
Carry me forth in the unknown
I am forever guided
By the love which you have sewn
Divine essence
Pure
And whole

The Memory

His holding me
In the rhythm of peace
And it's not a dream
When so clearly I see
The remembrance of his soul
In the morning
Nothing to be
Don't we all want nothing to be
But in purity
The way we came
I have forgotten
The motion that speaks
Only to me
In the days I live
For a little while
But when I am alone
Kisses placed
Upon my forehead
Where true intimacy remains
Breaking the silence
Of the eyes I have kept
Half asleep
And steady now
The light rises from their voices
Demure and quiet

The echo streams
Brushing all of my body
Again awake
I rise

Enchantment

I want to live
High above the tallest mountain
Where the cool crisp air
Kisses my cheeks
And the light is bright enough
To be a movement
To run his hands through my hair
Where the most crystal blue waters
Cascade through the beds
Beyond the largest live oak
Rooted deep
In the glimmering grain
Of stardust
And I rise
With bright wondering again
In all things again
That I do not know
And he has given me
The key
Only this time
Handed for deepest joy
In firmament
How could I have ever forgotten
The ocean
That I have not seen

In years
That I now fly upon light wings
To live by
In hues of turquoise and others
Rushing in
To kiss my ankles and toes
Where I safely lay
Warm and protected
Under a silver sun
That I view in wonder
Bringing me perfect warmth
For the rhythm
My new body craves
And as I close my eyes
My loves comes
Surprisingly
To brush the velvet rose
Upon my skin
In anticipation
For his touch again
As the moonbeams
Paint a glow
For he turned on the night
In the glimmer
Of his soft eyes
Melting with desire
Waiting
Upon lifetimes

Summertime

Was all lost for another
Or was she really making it count
When she shouldn't
She confessed in other words
Staying in his common rhythm
Because I am falling upon
The promise of another promise
And if I may
Make it so I float upon
Sheets pressed in lavender
With the finest silk upon my skin
Or am I just dreaming
He will be catching me there
Soft as the warmest touch
Sweet as honey upon my lips
Like he said
When he was pulling me in
In lack for the resolve
Of another hidden day
We kept
Tucked away from the world
Under a starry sky
Delicious as the berries
Growing wild
And as deep in their color
Staining summertime

Children

Children of the sun
Create the future you desire
To see for yourselves
Release the past
To a gale
Kiss the sunrise as it falls
At your feet
Embody the tides
Of your human existence
And learn to allow all emotions
To pass through you
Without becoming bound to them
Prioritize yourself and the goals
You have set for yourselves
Allow nothing to break
The sacred bond
You hold
And forever shall
Only for yourself
Don't give your heart away
To the world
Who will be forever
Desperately in need
Cry, laugh, sing, dance for joy
Weep with those who have wept

And above all
Give yourself
Grace
For every season of life
That has been yours
I love you
And believe in you forever

www.ingramcontent.com/pod-product-compliance
Lightning Source LLC
Chambersburg PA
CBHW051720130826
49812CB00034B/1268
9789357214261